Table of Contents

Introduction to Practical Exercises 3
    How the Practicals Work 3
    Group Work 3
    What to Bring With You 4
    Scheduling of Practicals 4
    Your Laboratory Notebook 4
    Evaluation 4
    Missed Practicals 4

Practical Session 1: Kinematics in One Dimension 6
    Exercise 1: Frame of Reference 7
    Exercise 3: Experimentally Verify a Prediction 9

Practical Session 2: Forces 10
    Exercise 1: Elements of a Free-Body Diagram 11
    Exercise 2: Free-Body Diagram of a Real Scenario 13
    Exercise 3: Free-Body Diagram of Cart on a Track – Making Predictions 14
    Exercise 4: Free-Body Diagram of Cart on a Track – Testing Predictions 15

Practical Session 3: Conservation of Energy 17
    Exercise 1: Mechanical Energy 18
    Exercise 2: Kinetic and Potential Energy 19
    Exercise 3: Experiment – Mechanical Energy 20

Practical Session 4: Waves, Superposition and Reflections **21**

    Exercise 1: Traveling Waves 22

    Exercise 2: Reflections at Boundaries..23

    Exercise 3: Waves on Waves 24

    Exercise 4: Standing Waves..26

Practical Session 5: Home Experiment and Video.. **28**

Appendix: Using *Data Studio*... **29**

Introduction to Practical Exercises

The practical component of Physics 1A03 is outlined in this manual. These exercises will be done in groups and provide hands-on, practical examples. The practicals provide ways of thinking about the lecture material, but they are not "laboratories" in the traditional sense of the word: you will not be asked to perform a classical experiment or verify a physics law, and you will not be asked to write up your experiment in terms of "Purpose", "Apparatus", "Method", etc. You *will* be asked to make predictions and then test them, and you *will* be asked to think about *why* some things occur. You want to look at the practical as an opportunity to explore physical ideas in a hands-on way. While this exploration will be guided by the questions in the manual, it can occur somewhat at your own pace and in your own directions.

How the Practicals Work

During your practical sessions, you will work in a group of, typically, 3 students on the exercises outlined in this manual. Some of these are "pencil-and-paper" exercises, in which you will make a prediction or verify some theoretical result. Others will involve making observations of some system which is set up in the laboratory, and still others will ask you to design an experiment to test a prediction. In all cases, these tasks are guided by questions posed in the manual, but the details for the steps required to come to a solution may not be spelled out in detail. The process of applying your physical knowledge to predicting, testing and verifying without direct instructions from the manual or your teaching assistants is the most important aspect of the practical sessions.

At the beginning of the term, some students find the teaching assistants to be frustrating. This is because the teaching assistants are not there to answer the questions in the manual. Ideally the teaching assistants are there to guide you to find the answers yourself: the teaching assistant's role is to help you solve the problem.

Group Work

The practical exercises, and physics research in general, is a collaborative experience. We expect and encourage you to discuss, question, and argue with your group members about these exercises. The most effective learning groups are ones where *all* members participate. As such, it is important to be a good group citizen. It is all too easy to let the most confident or outgoing member of a group set the pace. Don't let yourself be left behind! If you don't understand why the answer should be 5, say so. Similarly, be patient with your fellow students! In clarifying a point for someone else, you just may learn something.

What to Bring With You

For each practical session, bring:

- This manual.
- Your laboratory notebook in which you will answer the questions in the exercises and record your observations and questions. The bookstore carries "Physics Laboratory Notebooks", a bound notebook with a hard cover which includes graph paper. The notebook is yours, it is for you to keep a record of your activities and to use in your studies.
- A calculator.

Scheduling of Practicals

Practicals run roughly every other week unless otherwise noted in your course outline or in class.

Your Laboratory Notebook

The laboratory notebook is for your benefit. It is a record of all of the exercises performed during the practical. If it is to be useful to you when studying, it needs to be kept in a useful way. Write legibly, draw graphs on graph paper, put your "scratch work" on a separate page. When you take data, record it in such a way that if you were to look back on it a month later, you would still be able to figure out what you had measured (units are important). Ensure that you bring your notebook with you every practical session. Your teaching assistants may review your notebook with you in order to guide your learning.

Evaluation

The evaluation of the practical exercises will be based on your performance in the practical sessions, and questions on the term test and final exam. During the practical session, you must discuss your answers to each exercise with your teaching assistant, and the teaching assistant must sign off on each exercise before you can continue. Your laboratory notebook may be checked periodically.

On the term tests and final exam some questions will be drawn directly from the practical exercises or will ask about something that you investigated during the practical session.

Missed Practicals

If you miss a regularly scheduled practical for any reason, you should submit an MSAF form and then see the laboratory supervisor, Alex Vorobyov, as **soon as possible,** to arrange a time to makeup the missed work (normally within two weeks of the missed practical).

Practical Session 1: Kinematics in One Dimension

Set yourself the following objectives for this week's practical session:

> - Be able to clearly define, in words, the kinematic terms position, displacement, velocity, and acceleration.
> - Be able to describe the motion of an object moving along a line in terms of the kinematic variables.
> - Understand and be able to apply the sign conventions for velocity and acceleration.
> - Be able to interpret position vs. time, velocity vs. time, and acceleration vs. time graphs.

There are three exercises in this week's practical session. In Exercise 1, you will have an opportunity to work out the sign conventions for the kinematic variables. In Exercises 2 and 3, you will predict and then observe how the kinematic variables will behave as a function of time for a cart moving on a track.

Don't rush from one exercise to the next! It is better to understand one exercise than to be confused by three!

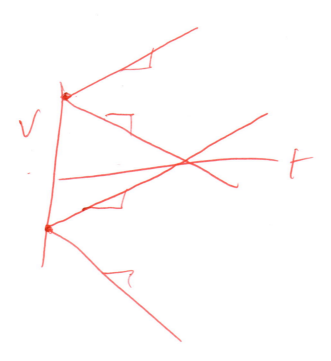

Exercise 1: Frame of Reference

At your desk, you should find a short piece of track with a motion sensor mounted at one end. You can adjust the tilt of the track using the **large screw on top** of the end support. Place the rolling cart on a nearly **level** track (see picture below).

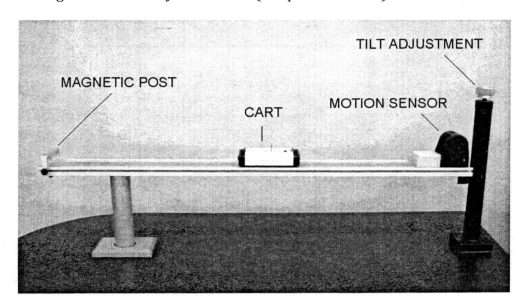

Launch **Data Studio** and open the file *motionsensor*. Press the start/stop button in the top left hand corner of the screen to begin/stop talking the data. As you move the cart around on the track, you will be able to observe how **Data Studio** plots the position, velocity, and acceleration as a function of time for the moving cart.

Discuss the following questions within your group. You will want to make notes in your laboratory notebook:

1.1 What is a reference frame? What is the reference frame assumed by the **Data Studio** software? **[HINT]**

1.2 The motion sensor measures the position of the cart at regular time intervals. It does not directly measure either the velocity or the acceleration. How then are the velocity and acceleration data arrived at? **[HINT]**

1.3 Move the cart in front of the motion sensor and look at the velocity-time graphs produced by **Data Studio**. In which direction is the cart moving when **Data Studio** shows a positive velocity? A negative velocity? Does the sign of the velocity depend on whether the cart is speeding up or slowing down?

1.4 How must the cart move in front of the motion sensor in order for **Data Studio** to show a positive acceleration? A negative acceleration? Use **Data Studio** to check your predictions. **[HINT]**

Discuss your observations with your teaching assistant before moving on.

Exercise 2: Graphing Position, Velocity, and Acceleration

2.1   Please **shut down *Data Studio*** for this exercise.

On a graphing page in your laboratory notebook, draw 3 large graphs, one underneath the other, as shown in the adjacent diagram. The first graph should show position vs. time, the second, velocity vs. time, and the third, acceleration vs. time. The time axes **must** be aligned.

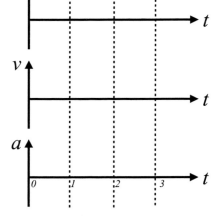

If the track is tilted, we can create the following scenario: A cart rolls **towards** the detector with a **decreasing** speed. The cart comes to rest instantaneously, and then moves away from the detector with increasing speed. **[SEE VIDEO]**

On your graphs, sketch what you think the position, velocity, and acceleration of the cart will look like as a function of time.

Once your group agrees on a set of sketches, show them to your teaching assistant.

2.2.1 Tilt the track system in a suitable way so as to reproduce the motion in exercise 2.1. Use ***Data Studio*** to measure the position, velocity and acceleration of this motion. Create a new set of sketches for the position, velocity and acceleration in your laboratory notebook (as you did in Exercise 2.1) and graph the Data Studio output. Compare the two sets of sketches (predicted vs. observed) and try to discern the error(s) in your original argument. **[SEE VIDEO]**

2.2.2 Recall that Newton's first law states that an object at rest will remain at rest unless acted on by an external force. What is the difference between an object being "at rest" in the sense of Newton's first law, and an object "coming to rest momentarily" as you observed in this exercise?

2.2.3 If you are told that an object has a positive acceleration, would you be able to determine if the object is speeding up or slowing down? If not, what further information would you require?

Discuss your results with your teaching assistant before moving on to the next exercise.

Exercise 3: Experimentally Verify a Prediction

3.1   Please **shut down *Data Studio*** for this exercise.

On a new page in your notebook, sketch 3 large graphs which show the position, velocity and acceleration as a function of time (as you did in the previous exercise). The time axes must be aligned.

Consider the following scenario: A cart is at rest on a level track. You give it a brief, strong push. It rolls along the track at a constant speed. At the far end of the track, it collides with the magnetic post and rebounds. **[SEE VIDEO]**

Sketch what you think the position, velocity, and acceleration as a function of time would look like for the moving cart. Start by dividing the time axis up into the time ranges: *before* the push, *during* the push, *while* the cart is *rolling*, the *collision* with the post, and the time *after* the collision. Label each of these events on your graph. Try to use time intervals that are appropriate to each event; e.g. the collision happens over a shorter time compared to the rolling time. Be sure to not make the time intervals too short! You want to have enough room to clearly sketch what you think is happening.

Once your group agrees on a set of sketches, show them to your teaching assistant.

3.2   Use ***Data Studio*** to verify your predictions. Click the start button, *wait several seconds* , and then give the cart a push and observe the collision. Draw a new set of sketches and graph the output from Data Studio. Compare these sketches with your predictions from earlier and try to discern the error(s) in your original argument.

Discuss your observations with your teaching assistant.

Practical Session 2: Forces

Set yourself the following objectives for this week's practical session.

- Be able to name and recognize the various forces that you come across in daily life. Give some thought to their underlying physical origin.
- Be able to construct free-body diagrams.
- Be able to identify contact forces and non-contact forces

There are four exercises in this practical session. Be patient! There are important points to be made in each exercise. The arguments are fundamental to solving dynamics problems! Take your time and come to terms with this material.

Exercise 1: Elements of a Free-Body Diagram

Einswine and Physics Girl are attempting to move a forklift. Einswine is pushing the forklift and Physics Girl is pulling a rope attached to the front as shown. The forklift is at rest.

1.1 In your notebook draw a free-body diagram for the forklift. Start with a large dot representing the forklift and draw vectors, with the tail of the vector on the dot and the tip pointing away, that represent the different forces acting on the forklift. Label each force.

A few important points:
  a) All forces arise from an interaction between two objects.
  b) All forces are defined by the object on which the force acts and the object that exerts the force i.e. in the case above, a pushing force is exerted *on* the forklift *by* Einswine.

1.2 Identify which object is exerting each force on the forklift for each of the forces that appear in your free-body diagram above.

Note:
  a) A free-body diagram should only contain the object or system of interest and the forces acting upon it.
  b) A free-body diagram does not include the forces exerted by the object or system of interest.

1.3 The interactions between objects can take different forms. In your notebook write down which of the forces that acted on the forklift required *direct contact* between the object exerting the force and the forklift (called *contact forces*)? Which did not (called *non-contact forces*)?

1.4 There are many kinds of forces: tension ($\vec{T}$), friction force ($\vec{f}$), normal forces ($\vec{N}$), gravitational forces ($\vec{W}$), magnetic force ($\vec{F}_{mag}$), etc. Make a table in your notebook and identify which are contact forces and which are non-contact forces.

1.5   For the following two sample conversations, which student, if any, do you agree with? Why?

    Student 1: "The free-body diagram for the forklift should have a force by Einswine, Physics Girl and the rope."

    Student 2: " The free-body diagram for the forklift should not have a force by Physics Girl. Physics Girl cannot exert a force on the forklift without touching it."

Once your group is done, show your free-body diagram to your teaching assistant.

Exercise 2: Free-Body Diagram of a Real Scenario

2.1   Draw at **a** free-body diagram for at least one of the real objects set up in the laboratory, one on each desk. If you wish to practice, feel free to try some of the other objects.

In each case:

- Make a reasonably **large** sketch (like the one on the description sheet) of the object for which the free-body diagram is required.
- Draw vectors which show the forces acting on the object. When drawing a vector describing a contact force, place the tail of the vector where the contact force is being applied (i.e. where the two objects touch).
- Now that you are back at your desk, would you like to revisit any of the objects? Pictures are available **[SEE VIDEO]**

Exercise 3: Free-Body Diagram of Cart on a Track – Making Predictions

3.1 A block (cart+sensor) is held **at rest** on a **frictionless** horizontal track. One end of a string is attached to the block and the other to a cylinder which is hung over a pulley as shown. A hand presses on an upper horizontal surface of the system.

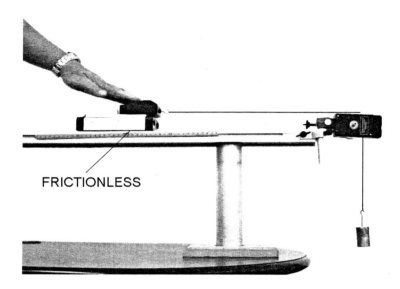

3.1.1 Draw a free-body diagram for the block and a separate free-body diagram for the cylinder, labeling the forces in the usual way. Assume that the tension is the same everywhere in the string and that the hand presses down on the system.

3.1.2 How does the magnitude of the tension in the string compare to

  a) the weight of the cylinder?
  b) the horizontal force exerted by the hand on the block?

  If necessary, modify your free-body diagram to reflect your conclusions.

3.1.3 What physical law did you use to compare the forces in part (b). Explain.

3.2 Suppose that the block is released:

  a) Draw new free-body diagrams. One for the block **and** one for the cylinder.
  b) How will the block and cylinder move when released?
  c) How does the magnitude of the tension in the string compare to the weight of the cylinder? What physical law did you use to compare the forces? Explain.
  d) What happens to the tension in the string when the block is released?

Exercise 4: Free-Body Diagram of Cart on a Track – Testing Predictions

With the **Data Studio** equipment, you can test the predictions made in the previous exercise. Open the **Data Studio** file called *forcesensor* and create a graph of force vs. time.

Set up the cart/track/pulley system as shown below.

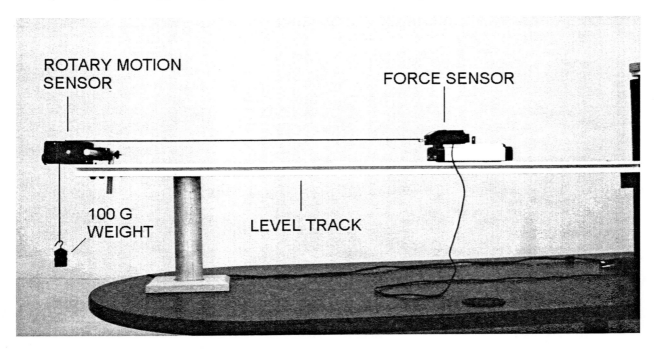

[SEE VIDEO]

The sensor will need to be calibrated before the measurement. There is a "tare" (or "zero") button on the top of the force sensor. Reduce the force on the probe to zero by holding the cylinder in your hand so that the string is not pulling on the probe. Click the start button on the viewer to observe the force and if the force measured is not zero, hit the tare button to zero it. After completing this task, press stop, delete the data and proceed with the following:

Hang the cylinder over the pulley and hold the cart still. **After you have recorded the force sensor reading for several seconds**, release the cart. Stop your data recording before the cart hits the foam barrier.

a) Which of the forces on your free-body diagram is the force sensor measuring? Is the force acting on the sensor while the cart is **at rest** consistent with your prediction? Calculate the force of gravity acting on the cylinder and see how it compares with the force on the sensor.
b) Is the behaviour of the force acting on the sensor while the cart is accelerating consistent with your prediction?

c) The mass of the cart+sensor and cylinder are provided. Use your free-body diagrams to calculate the **tension force** and the **acceleration** of the system, assuming that the track is level and that rolling friction is negligible. How do these predicted values compare to your measured values? To measure the values on data studio, first click and drag your mouse over the data you are interested in. A box will then appear which shows the average value of the data in that range. Note the measured values in your lab notebook.

Practical Session 3: Conservation of Energy

Set yourself the following objectives for this week's practical session:

- Be able to clearly define the term potential energy.
- Be able to calculate the potential energy associated with elastic and gravitational forces.
- Be able to apply conservation of energy to simple mechanical systems.

There are three exercises in this practical session allowing you to observe and interpret the energy transformations in an oscillating system. You will be using the **Data Studio** calculator in this session: you may want to review the relevant sections of the Appendix "Using **Data Studio**" before coming to the laboratory.

Exercise 1: Mechanical Energy

Please be careful! A spring which is stretched too far will be permanently deformed and unusable.

1.1 Set up the cart-spring-weight system as shown in the image below. The track should be level.

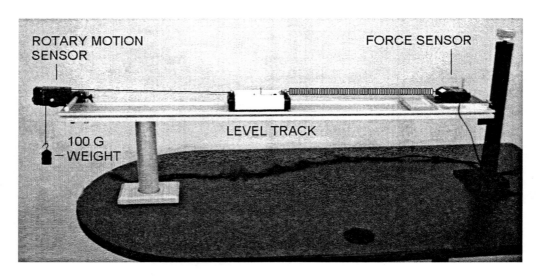

a) What is the definition of mechanical energy?
b) Set the cart-spring-weight system in motion and observe it. What kinds of energy would you associate with the system during the oscillation?
c) Write a complete expression for the total mechanical energy of the system. Your expression should include all known and measurable quantities (mass, position, velocity, etc.). Clearly define all of the variables in your equation (for example, in your lab notebook, write "M is the mass of the cart"). For clarity, use different symbols for the masses of different objects (i.e. the mass of the cart should be represented by a different variable than the mass of the weight).

1.2 Open the file *energy*.

You can measure the spring's force constant, k, using the force and rotary motion sensors. Measure the force and position curves as the cart moves. Then, drag the position data (from the panel on the left hand side of the screen) onto the horizontal axis of the force-time graph to create a force-position graph (make sure the horizontal axis is highlighted by a black box before you drop the data). Sketch the force as a function of position in your notebook. Determine the spring constant. **(HINT: you can easily measure the slope of a straight line in Data Studio by highlighting the data, going to the "Fit" drop down menu and selecting linear fit.)[SEE VIDEO]**

Exercise 2: Kinetic and Potential Energy

In this experiment, the motion of the cart will be monitored by a rotary motion sensor. The motion sensor works as follows. As the cart moves, the pulley rotates and an optical sensor in the pulley housing measures the angle that the pulley rotates. One complete rotation corresponds to a linear displacement equal to the circumference of the disc. The *Data Studio* software does the conversion from the angular to the linear measure for you.

a) Determine the reference frame used by the rotary motion sensor. How does it assign the origin? Which direction defines the positive axis? **[HINT]**

Move the cart as near to the force sensor as the barriers allow so that the spring is at its natural length (i.e. it isn't stretched or compressed). We will call this the initial configuration of the system.

b) If you start the run with the system in the initial configuration, what coordinate (i.e. x value) will the rotary motion sensor assign to the position of the cart or weight?
c) What is the spring's elastic potential energy in the initial configuration? Given the sensor's choice of reference frame, how would you write an equation, in terms of the measured position (x), which describes the potential energy of the spring as a function of position?
d) Given the sensor's choice of reference frame, how would you write an equation, in terms of the measured coordinate, which describes the gravitational potential energy of the weight? Check that your equation is consistent with the fact that the weight will lose gravitational potential energy as it falls. What then is the initial gravitational potential energy?
e) If the cart is released from rest at this position, what is the initial total mechanical energy of the system? Does this seem reasonable?

Exercise 3: Experiment – Mechanical Energy

3.1   Again, move the cart as near to the force sensor as the barriers allow, so that the spring is at its natural length. Click the start button, wait several seconds, and then release the cart. Monitor its motion on *Data Studio* through several oscillations. In particular, **write down** how far the weight falls on the first descent (this will be your measured fall distance).

Is mechanical energy strictly conserved during the oscillation? What evidence supports your answer? **[HINT]**

3.2   The formulas for the kinetic energy, gravitational potential energy, the spring potential energy, and the total mechanical energy have already been provided for you in *Data Studio*. **[SEE EXAMPLE]**

On a single graph in your laboratory notebook, carefully sketch the plot from *Data Studio* and label the measured energy functions over **one complete cycle** of an oscillation that begins with the spring un-stretched.

On your graphs, label where the cart is when each of the energies is at its maximum and minimum values. Label these points with letters A, B, C, etc. and draw a picture of the track labelling where A, B, C, etc. occur. **[SEE EXAMPLE]**

3.3   The plot of the total mechanical energy as a function of time shows that energy is being lost from the system. However, we may still be able to use conservation of mechanical energy to predict the motion of the cart-spring-weight system during the **first oscillation** since only a small fraction of the energy is dissipated over that time.

   a) What is the initial mechanical energy of the system?
   b) Write an expression, as a function of the variables x and v, which describes the mechanical energy at any subsequent time.
   c) Use conservation of mechanical energy to predict how far you would have expected the hanging weight to fall when the system was released. How does it compare to your measured value?
   d) How does the fall distance in (c) compare to the predicted distance the weight has to fall to reach the *equilibrium* position? You will have to perform a calculation to determine the equilibrium position. **[HINT]**

Practical Session 4: Waves, Superposition and Reflections

Set yourself the following objectives for this week's practical session.

> - From observation, to develop an appreciation of what a traveling wave is.
> - Be able to write a mathematical description of a traveling wave.
> - To observe and note how a wave is reflected at a sudden change in the medium.
> - To understand what is meant by "linear superposition" and to test the principle by observation.
> - To be able to distinguish a standing from a traveling wave, and to know how to make a standing wave.

This practical contains four exercises.

The trouble with waves is that they come and go before we get a chance to get a good look at them. We are going to start with observations of some waves which move fairly slowly so that we can see what goes on. We will then look at how two waves interact. The following is a script of observations that can be made. The teaching assistants can give additional help and explanation when you need it. Some of the observations have been video recorded, so that you can examine the motion in detail.

During the practical, you will be referred to various video clips. The list of available videos can be found in the folder *Video Files* on the desktop. The videos run on any Media Player. You can view the entire video by using the play button at the bottom of the screen. To look at any particular frame, use your mouse and manually drag the time indicator (slider) forward or backward.

Exercise 1: Traveling Waves

1.1   All of our waves will be forced to travel along a line of some description e.g. along a rubber hose, a coil spring, or a torsion line. The torsion line (which is waiting for you in the ante-room) is a flat strip of spring steel, hanging vertically, with cross-weights attached at equal intervals. The wave is a twisting disturbance, and the cross-weights assure a very low wave velocity.

You can observe a continuous wave traveling along the torsion line in the video clip:

   real traveling sine wave

For *this* clip, the torsion line has been set up in such a way that there is **no reflection** from the far end to confuse the observations.

Observe the clip. What happens to the shape of the disturbance as it travels? What is the wavelength of the disturbance? What is the period of the oscillation? Does the disturbance travel at a constant speed? Estimate the speed. **[HINT]**

Exercise 2: Reflections at Boundaries

2.1   As the wave travels, there is an orderly exchange of potential and kinetic energy along the medium. But what happens when the wave reaches the far boundary of the medium (e.g. the end of the torsion line)? If there is nothing there, or the termination is too massive and rigid to accept any significant energy, then the wave reverses upon itself in what we would call a "reflection".

A demonstration of a torsion line will be done for you once all the groups in the lab have finished with Exercise 1. If you have finished Exercise 1 and are waiting for the rest of the groups, you may move onto to the next Exercise 2.2 if you feel comfortable. During the demonstration, pay particular attention to what happens to a disturbance **after** it has reflected from the far end of the line. For the moment ignore what happens during the reflection: we will return to this in the next exercise.

When you return, you will be able to review the arguments using the video clips.

2.2   It turns out that how the wave is reflected depends on how the line is terminated. Begin with the video clip:

real pulse 1 reflection

Here you will observe a short pulse created at the top of the torsion line which travels to the bottom of the line and is reflected there. In this case, there is nothing constraining the torsion line at the bottom. The boundary is said to be "free".

In what ways are the incident and reflected pulses similar? In what ways are they different?

2.3   Now, move on the to the video clip:

real pulse 2 reflections

In this clip, the pulse will be reflected twice, once from the bottom (again a free end) and once from the top. The top end, however, is constrained: the steel strip is rigidly attached to the post and unable to move. This boundary is said to be "fixed".

In what ways are the incident and reflected pulses (from the fixed end) similar? In what ways are they different?

Discuss your results with your teaching assistant before moving on to the next section.

Exercise 3: Waves on Waves

3.1 So far, we have looked at individual wave disturbances. In this section we want to address the question: "What do we observe when two waves overlap?"

Let us consider the simplest way of adding up disturbances and then see if it is consistent with our observations. Linear superposition states that if effect E alone produces result E, and effect F alone produces result F, then both effects acting at the same time will produce result E plus result F. This is demonstrated in a video simulation. This video shows the superposition of a triangular pulse and a rectangular pulse travelling through a medium in opposite directions. Before playing the video, can you predict, using the principle of linear superposition, how the wave form will evolve with time?

superposition simulation

3.2 Let us now take a closer look at the time interval during a reflection. Consider the following scenario:

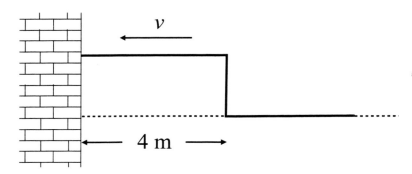

A rectangular pulse, 4 m long, is incident on a fixed boundary as shown in the diagram. The pulse is traveling at 1 m/s and is shown at $t = 0$, just as it makes contact with the wall.

Because the pulse is 4 m long, the back end of the pulse will not reach the wall for 4 s. During that 4 sec interval, the trailing edge of the pulse will continue traveling toward the wall while the leading edge will have undergone reflection and will be traveling away from the wall. Clearly there are two pulses, an incident and a reflected pulse, near the boundary, and they occupy the same space at the same time.

If linear superposition is correct, then we can analyze the waveform during the reflection by simply adding the incident pulse to the reflected pulse. We know what the reflection looks like from observations **after** the reflection interval.

On a fresh page in your laboratory notebook, sketch a series of graphs (5 in total), which show $y(x)$ for the rectangular pulse described above, at $t = 0, 1, 2, 3$, and 4 sec. The graphs should be to scale, and their axes aligned. At each time, sketch the forms of the incident and reflected pulses and then sketch the total wave (incident + reflected) using the principle of superposition to add them up. You may want to use different colours for your incident, reflected and total waves.

Once you have a prediction for the behaviour of the pulse during the reflection, look at the complete video simulation of the event:

pulse reflection simulation

Describe, in words, how the waveform evolves after reflection from the boundary.

3.3 It is possible to observe what really happens to a long pulse reflected from a fixed boundary using the torsion line? You can generate a pulse which starts at the bottom of the line and is reflected from the top. If the pulse is made almost as long as the line itself, there is a long period of time over which the upward moving pulse and its reflection overlap. A video clip is also available:

real pulse reflection and simulation

Is the waveform consistent with your prediction based on linear superposition?

Have your teaching assistant look over your results before you go on.

Exercise 4: Standing Waves

4.1   A standing wave is another case of wave superposition of considerable importance. The conditions for the creation of a standing wave are demonstrated in the simulation:

standing wave simulation

In this case a "green" wave and a "blue" wave superpose to create a "red" wave. You can stop the video at any time and convince yourself that the red wave displacement is the sum of the blue and green wave displacements.

In what ways are the green and blue waves similar? In what ways are they different? Consider as many wave properties as you can think of.

In what ways are the red and blue waves similar? In what ways are they different?

Notice that in a standing wave, there are places where the sum of the two waves is always zero. These are called *nodes*. Places where the two waves add up to give an oscillation with the maximum possible amplitude are called *antinodes*.

4.2   It may occur to you that the condition for the creation of a standing wave is rather artificial. After all, how often does it happen that two identical waves travel through each other in opposite directions? Watch the video clip:

real standing wave

Would you recognize this as a standing wave? What specific features of the wave let you identify it?

We have seen that a standing wave is created when two identical waves travel through each other in opposite directions. In this case, what is the origin of the wave traveling to the left? What is the origin of the wave traveling to the right?

4.3   A boundary has an additional effect in that it imposes a condition on the vertical displacement of the wave at the boundary. What must the displacement for the standing wave be at the fixed boundary? At a free boundary?

4.4   With the equipment at your station, you will be able to create standing waves on a string attached to a vibrator at one end, and held in place at the other by a weight hung over a pulley.

Open the **Data Studio** file *Vibrator* on your desktop and check that your string vibrator is properly connected to the Pasco interface. Flip the red power switch on top the vibrator to the on position. **[SEE VIDEO]**

The "Signal Generator" dialogue box controls the oscillation frequency of the vibrator. At the moment, it should be set to 39 Hz. Use the Start/Stop toggle to set the vibrator oscillating. You should observe a reasonably strong three-loop standing wave on the cord. Optimize the wave by changing the length of the cord: loosen off the screw holding the vibrator to the track and shift the vibrator box a little to the left or right until you find the position at which the amplitude is a maximum. Once you are happy with the position, tighten the screw again.

Make whatever measurements are necessary on your standing wave in order to calculate the *wave velocity* of the traveling waves which superpose to create it.

4.5   You can change the frequency of the string vibrator either by typing a new frequency into the dialogue box or by using the +/− buttons (under the frequency input box) to step the frequency up or down in units of 1 Hz.

Increase the frequency 1 Hz at a time. What happens to the standing wave pattern? Why?

4.6   Continue to increase the frequency until you've detected two more standing wave resonances. How are the resonant frequencies related to each other? What is the next highest frequency at which a resonance will occur? At what frequency would the fundamental occur?

Choose one of the higher frequency resonances and recalculate the velocity of the component traveling waves. How does it compare to the result of **4.4**? Why?

Discuss your observations with your teaching assistant.

Practical Session 5: Home Experiment and Video

In groups of 2 or 3 prepare a demonstration or experiment at home with whatever materials you have. Then, make a short (5 minute maximum) video of the experiment or demonstration and explain the physics involved. Here you might want to think of the many demonstrations and experiments that Sara, Mike and Kari did in the modules. Be creative, have fun with it, and show us your best! We have expanded the scope of this "Home Experiment" and you can choose any topic we cover in class or any of the Modules. More information about this assignment and how to submit it will be available closer to the end of term.

Appendix: Using *Data Studio*

Where do I start?

You will be using a software package known as **Data Studio** for collection and analysis of much of your data in this course. Begin by familiarizing yourself with some of the more useful data-handling features of the software:

- Activate **Data Studio** by double-clicking the icon on the screen.
- Choose Open Activity from the menu.
- Double-click the file practice in the dialogue box that appears.

Once loaded, a graph viewer will appear and display a typical set of position vs. time data.

Wouldn't it be better to have the data fill the whole viewer?

Absolutely! There are two ways to expand the scale:

There is a white **scale-to-fit** button in the top left hand corner of the graph toolbar. Click on it and the axes will automatically scale so that the data fills the plot area.

Alternatively, you can use the cursor stretch function. Move your mouse pointer over any of the time values beside the title axis. The pointer will turn into the "stretch" cursor. With the left mouse button depressed, drag the cursor to the right or left to expand or compress the scale. The stretch cursor will operate on either axis.

Get into the habit of using the **scale-to-fit** stretch functions on every data set!

Sometimes, when using the stretch cursor, the data that you want to look at is stretched right off the viewer! Move your mouse pointer over either line representing the axes, and it will turn into a "hand" cursor. With the left mouse button depressed, drag the hand cursor left/right or up/down and the axes will follow. The hand cursor can also be used for moving information boxes on the graph viewer.

Suppose that I want to look carefully at some subset of the data?

This happens frequently. Move the mouse pointer into the graph area. Depress and hold the left mouse button down as you drag the cursor over the region that you wish to see on an expanded scale. Any data inside the box will be highlighted. Release the mouse button, and click on the **scale-to-fit** button. The highlighted portion of the data will now fill the viewer.

To retrieve the entire data set, click once, anywhere in the plot area, to clear the data selection, and then use the **scale-to-fit** button.

I suppose that there is some way to remove the plot from the viewer

Actually, several ways, but the keyboard delete key is the easiest. Click anywhere in the plot area and then use the delete key.

What is the rest of this stuff on the screen?

To the left of the graph viewer is the Data box which lists all of the data collected during the experiment. At the moment, it shows a single data set: the position, the velocity and the acceleration of a moving object as a function of time. If you click on the triangle to the right of the word Data, a drop down menu will appear. Click on "by Run" to organize the data by trial number. You may find this organization more useful when you have accumulated many sets of data

Can I plot any of this data?

Sure. Suppose that you want to plot the position vs time data. Move your pointer over to the data set called *Position Ch 1&2*. With the left mouse button depressed, you can drag it to the graph viewer. Release the mouse button and the plot will appear.

But I've seen this data set before. Can I see the velocity data?

Sure, but you have several options for viewing. The form of the plot will depend on **where you release** the mouse button on the viewer. Try this. Drag the velocity data onto the viewer and **keep the mouse button depressed as you move the pointer around the plot area**. Notice that when the pointer is near an axis (either one), a dashed box will surround that axis. When the mouse is away from the axes, the dashed box will surround the entire plot area. There are then three possibilities.

- If you release the mouse button while the box is around the vertical axis, the velocity vs time data will simply replace the position vs time data.
- If you release the mouse button while the box is around the horizontal axis, the velocity data will replace the time data and you will end up with a plot of position vs velocity.
- If you release the mouse button while the box surrounds the entire plot area, you will have two plots in the viewer: position vs time and velocity vs time.

Try one of everything and convince yourself that this is what happens!

Next?

I'm not sure what's in your viewer at the moment. Let me suggest that you replace it with three graphs: position, velocity, and acceleration for Run#1 as a function of time.

Done.

Did you notice that each set of data came up on its own graph? ***Data Studio*** recognizes that the units of the three data sets are all different (i.e. m, m/s, and m/s^2) and so plots them separately. If you had a second set of position vs. time data, for example, then ***Data Studio*** would plot it on the same graph as position vs time for Run#1.

Wouldn't the graphs be easier to compare if all of the time axes lined up?

Good point! On the graph tool bar, there is an **Align Axes** tool. Click on it once to activate it.

How do I remove a plot from the viewer now that there's more than one?

Notice that along with each data set plotted in the viewer, there is a description box, e.g.

> Acceleration Ch 1&2 Run #1

If you are in the graph viewer, one of the description boxes will be highlighted. To remove any data set, you can click on its description box in the graph viewer and then use the keyboard delete key. Try removing the acceleration data this way. Notice that the entire graph disappears.

Another useful option is to go to the **Data** menu on the **graph** toolbar (**not** the **Data** list on the left side of the screen). When you click on it, a drop-down toggle menu will appear. Any run with a checkmark beside it is displayed in the viewer. Click on a run to remove the checkmark. Notice that the data set disappears from the viewer, **but the graph remains**. This is useful when you want to see a plot of your data as it is being collected.

You can restore the position data to the viewer by returning to the toggle menu and clicking on Run#1 again.

Is there any way to get the numerical values for the data points off the graph?

Of course. Just to be definite, let us consider the position vs time graph. Click the **Smart Tool** button on the graph toolbar and a crosshair will appear on your graph together with the coordinates of the point (t, x) at the centre of the crosshair. Move your mouse pointer onto the origin of the crosshair and it will turn into a "hand" cursor with two axes attached. With the left mouse button depressed you can drag the hand cursor anywhere in the plot area.

Notice that if you move the cursor near to a data point, the cursor will lock on to it and provide you with the values of the measured time and position.

Sometimes you would like to see more decimal places in the reported values. If you go to the Data list on the left-hand side of the screen, and double-click *Position Ch 1&2*, for example, a properties box will appear. One of the options that you can set is the precision. Increase the precision to 4 decimal places. The **Smart Tool** will automatically adjust its reporting.

Clicking the **Smart Tool** button again, will turn it off.

There are other buttons on the graph toolbar. What do they do?

Slope Tool calculates the slope at any point on the graph using nearest neighbour points. Click on the Slope Tool button. Often a message appears asking you if you want to rescale the axes. We have never found it to be necessary. Just click No and continue. A short dark line will appear somewhere along your curve. Move your pointer along the line and it will eventually turn into a "hand" cursor. You can then click and drag the hand cursor to any point along your graph and read the slope.

Click the **Slope Tool** button again to turn off the function.

The **Fit Tool** lets you quickly compare your data to various functional forms. Click the **Fit Tool** button and a drop-down menu of possible forms will appear. When you click on **Linear Fit**, for example, a "best-fit" line, together with an information box which tells you the slope and intercept of the line, will appear on your graph.

Now, your particular data set may not be well-described by a straight line. However, as every experimenter knows, any set of data considered over a small enough region looks pretty well linear. Choose a subset of the data. The fit function will automatically adjust to that subset.

To turn off the fitting function, click the **Fit Tool** and either **Linear Fit** or **No Curve Fits**. You can experiment with other fitting functions if you'd like.

The **Analysis Tool** has many options. Click on the **Analysis Tool** button and a drop down menu will appear. Any function with a checkmark beside it is activated. The **Analysis Tool** will operate on an entire data set or on a selected subset of the data. Two of the more useful features are the *mean* function and the *area* function. Try them out.

Using the Calculator

Let's suppose that you have measured the velocity of a moving object, but are really interested in its kinetic energy. The kinetic energy and velocity are related by

$$K = \frac{1}{2} mv^2$$

The calculator allows you to define a kinetic energy function which operates on the velocity data as follows. The calculator button is located on the toolbar above the graph viewer. Click on it and a dialog box will appear. Delete whatever is in the entry box and type this instead, where we have assumed that the mass is 0.450 kg:

K = .5 *.450 *v^2 [enter]

Since the calculator does not recognize that K is the kinetic energy and that v is the velocity, you need to guide it. If you look below the row of buttons under the entry box, you'll see that it is asking you to define v. Go to the Data table (on the left hand side of the graph viewer). Use the drop down menu to arrange your data by *measurement*. Now drag *Velocity Ch 1&2* over to the calculator and drop it on *Please define variable "v"*.

What about the function K? The calculator allows you to attribute properties to the defined function, such as units and precision. Click on the Properties button and a dialog box appears. You can assign K the units of J for Joules. To complete the definition, you have to click on the **Accept** button. Notice that a new set of data, K, will appear in the **Data** list. You can now plot this data just as you would any of the original data.

Why did I have to arrange the data by measurement before using it in the calculator?

When the data is arranged *by run*, you have to choose a **specific** set of data, e.g *Velocity Ch 1&2 Run#l*. The kinetic energy function will then only be defined for Run#l. If you collect another set of data, you will have to re-enter the calculator and define the kinetic energy function for it.

If you organize the data *by measurement*, you have the option of using the general *Velocity* heading and the calculator will automatically do the calculation for each new data set.

OK. I feel ready to try an experiment now!

Great! First you need to get out of this activity file. Click on the **File** option at the top of the screen and choose **Open Activity**. When the dialogue box appears, double-click the *motionsensor* file. There will also be a rotarymotionsensor file for later use.

The Experiment Setup window allows you to choose the measuring apparatus to be used in an experiment and to set various operating parameters for them. For this session, we have taken care of those details for you. All you need to do is connect the motion sensor to channels 1&2 on the interface (yellow plug in channel 1) as shown in the setup window. After that, you can minimize the window.

The software offers several options for viewing the data. These are listed under the heading Display on the left-hand side of the screen about halfway down. Double-click the **Graph** option to open the graph viewer. You will probably want to enlarge your viewer.

Just to make sure that everything is working, set the motion sensor on the desk. Click on the **Start** button (near the top left-hand corner of the screen) and move your hand around in front of the sensor. The sensor may take several seconds to activate: the measurement begins when it starts clicking. Notice that the **start** button has become a **stop** button. After you click it, the data from this trial run will appear in the data list.

You can take more data by clicking the **start** button again. Obviously this is a way in which you can generate a lot of data! There are two ways to delete data from the list:

1. Move to the Data list. If your data is organized by run, click on the run that you want to remove and use the keyboard delete key.
2. At the very top of the screen, there is an Experiment options menu. The menu gives you the option of deleting the last run (useful when a measurement goes wrong right from the start) and deleting all runs – which should be used with some caution.